THE
INVISIBLE
FORCE

Also by Dr. Wayne W. Dyer

Meditations for Manifesting
The Power of Intention (abridged)
A Promise Is a Promise (audio book)
10 Secrets for Success and Inner Peace
The Secrets of the Power of Intention (6-CD set)
There Is a Spiritual Solution to Every Problem
The Wayne Dyer Audio Collection/CD Collection
Your Journey to Enlightenment (6-tape program)

<u>VIDEOCASSETTES</u>
Creating Real Magic in Your Life
How to Be a No-Limit Person
The Miracle Mindset
10 Secrets for Success and Inner Peace
What Do You Really Want for Your Children?

<u>MISCELLANEOUS</u>
Inner Peace Cards
Inspiration Cards
The Power of Intention Cards
The Power of Intention Perpetual Flip Calendar
10 Secrets for Success and Inner Peace Cards
10 Secrets for Inner Peace gift products:
Notecards, Candle, and *Journal*

All of the above are available at your
local bookstore, or may be ordered by visiting:

Hay House USA: **www.hayhouse.com**®
Hay House Australia: **www.hayhouse.com.au**
Hay House UK: **www.hayhouse.co.uk**
Hay House South Africa: **orders@psdprom.co.za**
Hay House India: **www.hayhouseindia.co.in**

THE
INVISIBLE
FORCE

365 Ways to Apply the Power of Intention to Your Life

DR. WAYNE W. DYER

LIFE *Styles*

HAY HOUSE, INC.
Carlsbad, California
London • Sydney • Johannesburg
Vancouver • Hong Kong • New Delhi

The material in this book was adapted from *The Power of Intention Perpetual Flip Calendar*, by Dr. Wayne W. Dyer (Hay House, Inc., 2004).

Library of Congress Control Number: 2005939098

ISBN: 978-1-4019-1195-9

10 09 08 07   4 3 2 1
1st printing, August 2007

Printed in Singapore

INTRODUCTION

I've put together this little book because I'd like to convey the fact that intention is a field of energy that flows invisibly beyond the reach of our normal, everyday habitual patterns. It's a force that we all have within us, and we have the power to draw it into our lives by *being* the energy we want to attract.

I hope you'll use the uplifting material within these pages to bring the power of intention into *your* life for many years to come, and experience the world in a new and exciting way!

— **Dr. Wayne W. Dyer**

The power of intention is the power of love and receptivity. It asks nothing of anyone, it judges no one, and it encourages others to be free to be themselves.

2

At our Source, we are formless energy, and in that vibrating spiritual field of energy, intention resides.

When life appears to be working against you, when the supposedly wrong people show up, or when you slip up and return to old, self-defeating habits, recognize the signs that you're out of harmony with intention.

4

Remain humble and grateful for all your accomplishments, and know that a force greater than your ego is always at work in your life.

By staying with the
higher energies of optimism,
forgiveness, understanding,
reverence for Spirit, creativity,
serenity, and bliss, your own
purpose—which revolves
around serving others and
serving God—becomes fulfilled,
and as a bonus, you create allies.

6

Meditation allows you to make conscious contact with your Source and regain the power of intention.

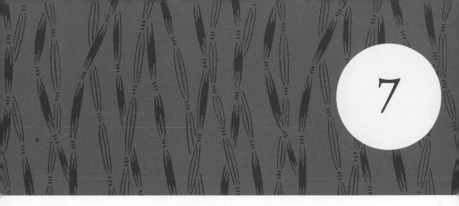

As you awaken to your divine nature, you'll begin to appreciate beauty in everything you see, touch, and experience.

8

y banishing doubt and

thinking in no-limit ways, you

clear a space for the power of

intention to flow through you.

Opening to the power of intention, you begin *knowing* that conception, birth, and death are all natural aspects of the energy field of creation.

10

Kindness extended, received, or observed beneficially impacts the physical health and feelings of everyone involved.

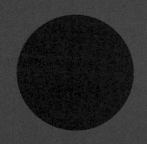

By choosing to see beauty
in everything, even a person
who is born into poverty
and ignorance will be able
to experience the power
of intention.

The words that represent the
seven faces of intention are:
creative, kind, loving, beautiful,
expanding, abundant, and
receptive. Memorize them to
bring yourself into harmony
with the power of intention.

*C*onsider being like a
mirror, and reflect what
comes into your life
without judgment or
opinions.

14

Your purpose will only be found in service to others, and in being connected to something far greater than your body/mind/ego.

*E*very thought you
have can be energetically
calibrated, along with its
impact on your body and
your environment.

Know that no one is capable of making you upset without your consent.

Arrange photographs of nature scenes, animals, and expressions of joy and love in your environment, and let their energy radiate into your heart and provide you with their higher frequency.

Rather than using language indicating that your desires may not materialize, speak from an inner conviction that communicates your profound and simple knowing that the universal Source supplies everything.

The power of intention is so doubt deficient that when you're connected to it, you see what you'd like to have as already being present.

20

Rather than praying to God
or a saint for a miracle, pray
for the miracle of an inner
awakening, which will never
leave you.

Make yourself available
for success, and know and
trust in an invisible force
that's all-providing.

22

$\mathcal{V}$iew the events you

consider obstacles as

perfect opportunities

to test your resolve and

find your purpose.

When you feel the need to have the right person show up in your life, affirm: *I know the right person is arriving in divine order at precisely the perfect time.*

24

Whatever you wish to accomplish is an existing fact that's already present in Spirit.

Look into a mirror, make eye contact with yourself, and say, "I love me" as many times as possible during the day.

Because it's omnipresent,
the energy field of intent is

completely accessible to you

after your physical arrival here

on Earth. The only way you

can deactivate this force is by

believing that you're separate

from it.

*C*ommunicate your views by being in harmony with the creative energy of the Source. You'll never be offended, because your ego won't be involved in your opinions.

28

See all so-called bizarre coincidences surrounding your desires as messages from your Source, and act upon them immediately.

29

The very fact that we can breathe and experience life is proof that the nature of the life-giving Spirit is creative at its core.

Treat yourself as if

you already are what

you'd like to become.

By retreating from low-energy substances such as alcohol and drugs, you can achieve the level of consciousness you crave.

Do not judge yourself or others for being too fat, too tall, too ugly—too anything! Just as the power of intention accepts and reflects you without judgment or attachment, try to be the same with what appears in your life.

Radiate an energy of serenity and peace so that you have an uplifting effect on those you come into contact with.

34

Whether you call it God, Spirit, Source, or intention, be aware that unkind thoughts weaken, and kind thoughts strengthen, your connection to it.

Your physical self is inspired by a divine force that beats its heart, digests its food, and grows its fingernails; and this same force is receptive to endlessly abundant health.

36

Remind yourself to be kind toward yourself in all the choices you make about your daily life.

Feelings of passion, pure bliss, reverence, optimism, trust, and illumination indicate that your desire to manifest success and abundance has an extremely strong pulling power from the universal Source to you.

38

Accept the fact that you'll never get it all done, and begin to live more fully in the only moment you have—now!

*S*ay to yourself, *I am here on purpose, I can accomplish anything I desire, and I do it by being in harmony with the all-pervading creative force in the universe.*

Strive to live with good cheer and kindness. That's a much higher energy than sadness or malevolence, and it makes the manifestation of your desires possible.

Refuse to see yourself as inauthentic or cowardly, because those thoughts will keep you from acting on what you know you were meant to be. Take daily steps to bring your thoughts of your grand heroic mission into harmony with your activities.

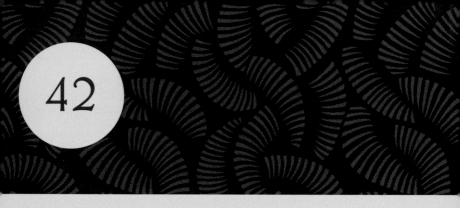

42

Avoid low-energy fields where there's excessive alcohol, drug consumption, or violent behavior, and gatherings where religious or ethnic exclusion and vitriolic prejudice are the focus.

*R*emember that your impact on others—whether strangers, family members, co-workers, or neighbors—is evidence of the strength of your connection to the power of intention.

44

By acting as if you're on

purpose and treating hurdles

as friendly reminders to

trust in what you feel deeply

within you, you'll be fulfilling

your own intention to be a

purposeful person.

*R*emember: You were intended out of love, so you must *be* love in order to intend.

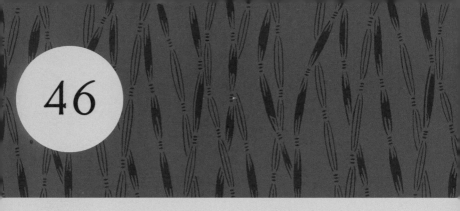

Say the word *intent* or *intention* repeatedly when you're in a state of anxiety or when everything around you seems to have conspired to keep you from your mission. This is a reminder to be peaceful and calm.

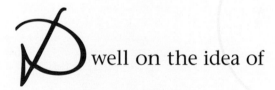well on the idea of

a supreme infinite power

producing the results you desire.

This is the creative power of the

universe.

48

hen people feel beautiful,

they act in beautiful ways.

Beauty proliferates in others just

by virtue of your presence when

you're connected to intention.

View those tenacious thoughts that just won't go away as intention talking to you, saying, "You signed up to express your unique brilliance, so why do you keep ignoring it?"

50

If others aren't treating you as you'd like, acknowledge: *I've taught these people how to treat me as a result of my willingness to make their opinions of me more important than my own. It's now my intention to teach them how I wish to be treated from here on in!*

You're not what you have

and you're not what you do;

you're an infinite, divine being

disguised as a successful person

who has accumulated a certain

amount of material possessions.

52

Know in your heart that seemingly miraculous happenings are brought into your immediate life space because you're already connected to them.

If you feel weak, lethargic, and fatigued after eating certain things, take note of what you've eaten so you can avoid eating these same low-energy foods in the future.

54

The quickest method for understanding and living your purpose is to ask yourself if you're thinking in loving ways.

What you feel is wrong or missing in your relationships is an indication that something is amiss within *you*.

Let go of the idea that
you're a body that's
destined to die, and
instead, seek an awareness
of your immortal self.

Place positive affirmations
in strategic places where
you'll notice and read
them throughout
the day.

The idea of extending kindness to others is particularly relevant in how you deal with people who are helpless, elderly, mentally challenged, poverty stricken, disabled, and so on. These people are all part of God's perfection.

Feel the surge of the life force that allows you to think, sleep, move about, digest, and even meditate. The power of intention responds to your appreciation of it.

60

Remember that every single modern advance you see and take for granted was created by someone contemplating what they intended to manifest.

Stressful, resistant thoughts don't have to be your habitual way of reacting to your world. By practicing thoughts of minimal resistance, you'll eventually become the tranquil person you wish to be.

62

Every aspect of nature, without exception, has intention built into it . . . the acorn never turns into a pumpkin, or the apple blossom into an orange.

Persistently viewing others
as dishonest, lazy, sinful,
and ignorant can be a way of
compensating for something
you fear.

64

Stay consistently matched up with the field of intention, and then watch for clues that what you're summoning from the all-creative Source is arriving in your life.

If you've ever felt inspired by a purpose or calling, you know the feeling of Spirit working through you.

66

If you desire peace for others, you'll receive it. If you want others to feel loved, you'll be the recipient of love.

*E*ven if it's only for a two-minute respite during which time you're silent, periodically concentrate on the name of the divine, or repeat the sound of "Ahh" as an inner mantra.

68

By allowing ego to determine your life path, you deactivate the power of intention.

69

Make it a point to use your free time to read about people who are examples of purposeful living, and model yourself after them.

By seeing yourself
as an infinite being, the
fear of death is forever
eliminated.

When you're not in harmony with the *energy* of love, you've moved away from intention and have weakened your ability to activate it through the *expression* of love.

72

If you're overly concerned

with how you're going to be

perceived by everyone, then

you've disconnected yourself

from intention and allowed the

opinions of others to guide you.

Quietly retreat from loud,

bellicose, opinionated people.

Send them a silent blessing and

then unobtrusively move along.

Practice kindness and goodwill toward all animals, tiny and huge; the entire kingdom of life on Earth, such as the forests, the deserts, and the beaches; and all that has the essence of life pulsating through it.

Love is cooperation rather
than competition, and
is the force behind the
will of God.

76

Don't absorb the weakening energies put out by those around you. Other people can't bring you down if you're operating at the higher energies.

Negative emotions tell you that your pulling power from intention is weak or even nonexistent; positive emotions tell you that you're connecting to and accessing the power of intention.

*R*emind yourself that

when you think about what

you resent, you act upon

what you think about, while

simultaneously attracting more

of it to you.

Greater Memphis ARTES Council

FUND FOR THE ARTS

By feeling good throughout the day, you become an instrument of peace, and it's through this channel that you eradicate problems.

80

Through imagination, God brings everything into reality. Make this your new strategy as well.

Perhaps the surest way to happiness and fulfillment in life is to thank and praise your Source for *everything* that happens to you. Then, even when a calamity arises, you can be assured that you'll turn it into a blessing.

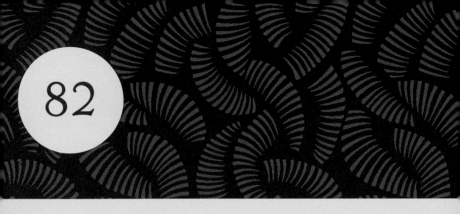

Make an internal
commitment to respect
yourself and feel worthy
of all that the universe
has to offer.

Become aware of your own amazing capacity to affect the healing and health of those around you simply by the silent presence of your high-energy connection to intention. This is a literal energy that emanates from you.

84

*B*egin practicing the intention to be authentic and peaceful with *everyone*. When you do so, you connect to peace itself.

See the light in others,
and treat them as if that
is all you see.

Raise yourself to the level of
energy where you *are* the light
you seek, where you *are* the
happiness you desire, where you
are the love you feel is missing,
where you *are* the unlimited
abundance you crave.

Your children are spiritual beings who come *through* you, not *for* you.

88

Believe in synchronicity.
Don't be surprised when
someone you've been thinking
about calls out of the blue,
when the perfect book arrives
unexpectedly in the mail, or
when the money to finance a
project mysteriously shows up.

There's always something beautiful to be experienced wherever you are. Right now, look around you and select beauty as your focus.

Match up with the "forthcomingness" of the universal mind from which everyone and everything originates while extending it outward, and you'll attract back to yourself all that you intend to manifest.

Simply refuse to think that you could be a victim of disease or disability, and do not spend the precious moments of your life discussing illnesses or past injuries.

$\mathcal{T}$ake some time to be silent, and repeat the sound of God ("Om" or "Ahh") as an inner mantra.

When you create a great longing for the experience of a peaceful family, everything will begin to happen to fulfill this yearning spontaneously and naturally.

Know that the universe is always

willing to work with you on

your behalf; and that you're

always in a friendly, rather

than a hostile, world.

Holy relationships facilitate
the power of intention at high
energy levels for everyone
involved. Unholy relationships
keep the energy at the lower,
slower levels for all concerned.

It's important to remember that hate, directed toward yourself or others, can always be converted into the life-giving, love-granting life force of intention.

Imagine that intention is not something you *do*, but rather a force that exists in the universe as an invisible field of energy.

You'll know your own potential for greatness when you start seeing the perfection in all relationships.

Train your thoughts to move at the levels of higher vibrations so that you're able to deflect lower/slower vibrations.

100

Anonymously perform acts of kindness, expecting nothing in return—not even a thank-you.

The way to establish a
relationship with Spirit and
access the power of this creating
principle is to continuously
contemplate yourself as being
surrounded by the conditions
you wish to produce.

102

Remember what philosopher Pierre Teilhard de Chardin said: "The conclusion is always the same. Love is the most powerful and still the most unknown energy of the world."

Make a conscious effort to shift to compassionate thoughts and feelings. For example, offer a silent blessing to the homeless rather than judging them as lazy or a drain on the economy.

When you hoard the abundance that arrives in your life, the flow is disrupted. You must keep it circulating, always knowing that nothing can stop it from coming into your life except any resistance *you* place in its way.

Hold no grudges and practice forgiveness. This is the key to having peace in all your relationships.

106

Spend some time observing babies. They don't work; they poop in their pants; and they have no goals other than to expand, grow, and explore this amazing world. Be like that baby you once were in terms of being joyful.

Seeking beauty in the
worst of circumstances
with individual intent
connects one to the
power of intention.

108

*P*ractice catching yourself when you have a thought of what others want for you, and ask yourself, *Does this expectation match up with my own?*

109

When the power of intention is working in your life, your presence will make others feel calm and assured.

Practice kindness toward Earth
by picking up a piece of litter
that's on your path; or saying
a silent prayer of gratitude for
the existence of rain, the color
of flowers, or even the book
you hold in your hands that
was donated by a tree.

Wisdom combined with discipline fosters your ability to focus and be patient as you harmonize your thoughts, your intellect, and your feelings with the work of your body.

Discarding doubt is a decision to reconnect to your original self. This is the mark of people who live self-actualized lives. They think in no-limit, infinite ways.

In order to attract and maintain romantic and spiritual partnerships, you must be what it is that you're seeking.

*E*ven in the worst situations,

you can process your world

with the energy of appreciation

and beauty, and create an

opportunity to transcend your

circumstances.

You may very well choose to

doubt what others say to you

or what you experience with

your senses, but banish doubt

when it comes to knowing that

a universal force of intention

designed you and got you here!

Cherish the energy you
share with all living beings
now and in the future—
as well as those who have
lived before you.

It's impossible to know and recognize your own perfection if you're unable to see and honor that same perfection in others.

The circumstances of your life aren't the way they are because of karmic debt or because you're being punished. These circumstances are simply yours, so just assume that you participated in all of them.

When you shift to an abundance mind-set, you repeat to yourself over and over again that you're unlimited because you emanated from the inexhaustible supply of intention.

The snow, the wind, the sun, and the sounds of nature can all be reminders to you that you're an integral part of the natural world.

By raising your energy to a vibrational match with the field of intention, you're strengthening your immune system and increasing the production of well-being enzymes in your brain.

Don't separate yourself

spiritually from anyone,

regardless of where they

might live or how different

their appearances or customs

may be from your own.

In order to float an idea

into your reality, you must be

willing to do a somersault into

the inconceivable and land on

your feet, contemplating what

you want instead of what

you don't have.

124

As you change your thought patterns to raise your energy vibrations, you'll begin developing a holy relationship with others, which is a way of matching up with the universal Source of Creation and being peacefully joyful.

As you appreciate your life force as representative of the power of intention, a wave of determination and knowing will surge through you.

126

*C*ommune with the Source in a

state of reverent gratitude for

all that's present in your life,

knowing that this empowers

your intention to manifest

precisely what you need.

The power of intention is everywhere. It is what allows everything to manifest, to increase, and to supply infinitely.

n an attitude of *allowing,*

all resistance in the form

of thoughts of negativity or

doubt are replaced with simply

knowing that you and your

Source are one and the same.

When you begin practicing the intention to be authentic and peaceful, you withdraw your consent to be in the lower energies.

Rather than being in a state of non-peace concerning any family members, say a prayer of gratitude for their presence in your life and all that they have come to teach you.

In any given moment of not feeling well, choose thoughts of healing and feeling good.

*B*eing hostile, hateful,
or angry toward people
who believe in and support
violence in any form will
only contribute to more of
that kind of debilitating
activity in the world.

Feeling abundant surpasses the money in your bank account and transcends what others may think of you.

Attempt to feel what would make others most happy and fulfilled. Then send the high energy of intention to that feeling, and concentrate on beaming this energy outward, particularly while in their presence.

If you disrespect anyone or anything that God creates, you disrespect that creative force and tarnish your connection to the power of intention.

If you're motivated to be
of service to others while
being authentically detached
from the outcome, you'll feel
"on purpose," regardless of
how much abundance
flows back to you.

Once you've accepted

your power to heal yourself

and optimize your health, you

become someone who's capable

of healing others as well.

If you're seeing yourself as

either inferior or superior,

you've disconnected from the

power of intention. Your desires

will be frustrated unless you

connect with and support

other people.

Love what you do and do what you love. It's that simple.

Become aware of your identification with "normal" or "ordinary," and begin to vibrate to higher and higher energetic frequencies, which constitute a shift upward into the extraordinary dimensions of pure intent.

Whatever it is that you want to do in life, make the primary motivation for your effort something or somebody other than your desire for gratification or reward.

142

When you can shift your inner thoughts to what *you* intend to create and attract into your life, you will no longer have to give mental energy to what others want for you.

Reject the concept of "enemies." Just know that all of us emanate from the same divine Source.

As you become acquainted with your eternal nature, you'll find yourself in a persistent state of gratitude for all that shows up. This state is the secret to fulfilling your own individual human intentions.

Wanting to feel good is synonymous with wanting to feel *God*. Remember: "God is good, and all that God created is good."

146

The secret to manifesting

anything that you desire is

your willingness and ability to

realign yourself so that your

inner world is in harmony with

the power of intention.

Know that there are many

possible outcomes for any

given condition, even for

those that may seem

impossible to overcome.

Let go of your ego's

need to be right.

The field of intention allows everything to emanate into form, and its unlimited potential is built into all that has manifested—even before its initial birth pangs were being expressed.

Watch your thoughts,
and when they're anything
other than compassionate,
change them!

If you ask with kindness in your voice and in your heart, "How may I serve you?" the universe's response will be, "How may I serve you as well?"

When you surrender, you
lighten up and can consult
with your infinite soul. Then
the power of intention becomes
available to take you wherever
you feel destined to go.

Avoid viewing anyone as ordinary, unless, of course, you wish to have more of the ordinary manifest into your own world.

Know that you don't have to ask for less, or feel guilty about wanting abundance—it's there for you and everyone in an unlimited supply.

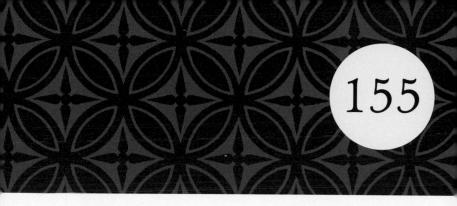

If there's a pattern within

you of seeing others as failures,

you need to notice this pattern

as evidence of what *you're*

attracting into your life.

156

As you follow the path of least resistance, success is no longer something you *choose;* it's something you *are.* Abundance no longer eludes you.

Rather than being interested in winning arguments, accumulating allies, and trying to persuade others to think as you do, be convincing through the positive energy you exude.

Begin noticing the
frequency of any thoughts
that support the idea of sickness
as something to be expected—
and eliminate them from
your mind.

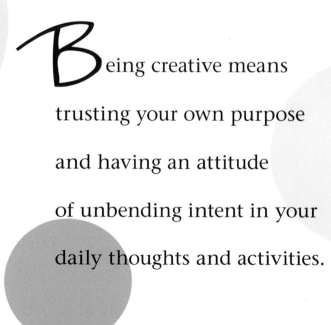

*B*eing creative means trusting your own purpose and having an attitude of unbending intent in your daily thoughts and activities.

$\mathcal{G}$enius is a characteristic
of the creative force that allows
all of material creation to come
into form. It is an expression
of the divine.

Have an absolute
knowing that you're in
vibrational harmony with
the all-creating force that
intended you here.

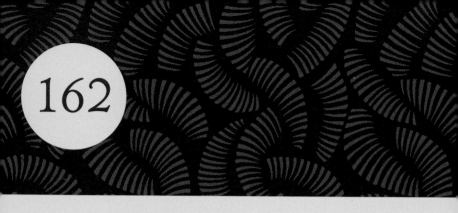

Be an appreciator
rather than a depreciator
of everything that shows
up in your life. Say "Thank
you, God" for everything.

The world of Spirit from which all is intended works in peace, love, harmony, kindness, and abundance, and that is where you can choose to reside within yourself.

164

The universal force of
intention never complains;
it creates, and offers its
options for greatness.

By seeing yourself as an infinite spiritual being having a human experience, rather than the reverse, the result will be a permanent connection to the abundance and receptivity of the universal Source that intends all of Creation into temporary form.

166

Be cognizant of the fact that you have the power to change the energy of your relationships with your family and friends through the power of intention.

Life itself is eternal, and you spring from this infinite *no thing* called life. Your ability to connect to the eternal and live in the here and now will determine whether you stay connected to the power of intention.

he ability to see yourself

in all of humanity is a

characteristic of the holy

relationship. It's the ability to

celebrate and honor in others

that place where we're all one.

Honor the physical temple that houses you by eating healthfully, exercising, listening to your body's needs, and treating it with dignity and love.

The stuff you own is not you. For that reason, you must avoid being attached to it in any way.

You *can* become proficient at raising your energy level and permanently obliterating energetic expressions that weaken or inhibit your connection to intention.

By being peaceful, quiet,
and receptive, you pattern
yourself in the image of God;
and you regain the power of
your Source.

It is only discord acting within your own feelings that will ever deprive you of every good thing that life holds for you. If you understand this simple observation, you'll curb interferences to intention.

$\mathcal{V}$iew the world as an abundant, providing, friendly place. If you do so, you'll see a world that wants you to be successful and abundant, rather than one that conspires against you.

Learn to be comfortable
with the concept of
infinity, and see yourself
as an infinite being.

Read the books that mysteriously show up in your life, and pay close attention to conversations that seem to indicate that you're being called to something new.

If left undisturbed in your mind
and in the mind of intention
simultaneously, what you desire
will germinate into reality in
the physical world.

Train your imagination (which

is the universal mind running

through you) to shift from

what you *don't* want to

what you *do* want.

Practice radical humility
when it comes to your
accomplishments, and
give credit everywhere
(except to your ego).

When the energies of
kindness, love, receptivity, and
abundance are present in your
relationships, you've brought
the love of the Creator right into
the mix.

The more you extend love—
even to those you feel have
harmed you in some way—the
closer you come to *being* love,
and it's in this beingness of love
that intention is reached.

182

If you're unwell, don't ask to be healed; instead, ask to be restored to that perfection from which you emanated.

Love creates new form,

changes matter, and

holds the cosmos together

beyond time and space.

It's in every one of us.

It's what God is.

If you could tap into the *feeling* of the power of intention, you'd sense that it is ever-increasing and confident in itself because it's a formative power so infallible that it never misses its mark.

Free will means that you have the choice to connect to Spirit or not.

186

In this universe, which
was created by a divine,
organizing intelligence,
there are simply no
accidents.

Remind yourself that by
raising your own energy
level to a place where you're
in harmony with intention,
you become an instrument,
or a channel, of peace.

188

Treat yourself and others with kindness when you eat, exercise, play, work, love, and everything else.

There are no accidents.
You're here for the purpose
that you signed up for
before you entered the
world of particles
and form.

*L*ink up with intention, use

your inner dialogue to stay

focused on what you intend

to create, and you'll find

yourself regaining the

power of your Source.

When you bring the frequencies of intention into the presence of others, they'll feel energized just by being in your immediate circle. You don't have to say a word.

It's an old concept, but it is nonetheless true: *We are all equal in the eyes of God.*

Simplify your life. Take the complications, rules, "shoulds," "musts," "have tos," and so on out of your consciousness.

You can either activate

thoughts that produce stress

within you, or activate thoughts

that make stress impossible.

It's your choice.

$\mathcal{E}$xpand your reality
to the point where you
pursue what you love
doing and excel at it.

It takes much more courage, strength of character, and inner conviction to forgive than it does to hang on to low-energy feelings.

When you're in the middle
of an argument, ask yourself,
Do I want to be right or be happy?
When you choose the joyous,
loving, spiritual mode, your
connection to intention is
strengthened.

If you don't believe that you're worthy of fulfilling your intentions for health, wealth, or loving relationships, then you're creating an obstacle that will inhibit the flow of creative energy into your daily life.

People who feel empowered by your presence become kindred spirits. That can only happen if they feel safe rather than attacked, secure rather than judged, calm rather than harassed.

When you practice
unbending intent,
you match up with the
intent of the all-creative
universal mind.

*R*efuse to allow your well-being to be affected by anything external to yourself—not the weather, not the wars someplace on the globe, not the economy, and certainly not anyone else's decision to wallow in low energy.

If you think you can't manifest abundance, you'll see intention agreeing with you, and *assisting* you in the fulfillment of meager expectations!

There are a million acts of kindness going on in the world at any given time. If you see yourself as a divine creation, you'll remember this as you view your surroundings, and the gloom-and-doom naysayers will have no impact on you.

204

*P*ractice being infinitely

patient, never being

dissatisfied with the

speed or the manner in

which your intentions

are manifesting.

Many relationships fail because one or both of the partners believe that their freedom has been compromised in some way. Spiritual partnerships, on the other hand, are never about making another person feel inferior or ignored in any fashion.

By shifting in the middle

of a weakening thought to

one that strengthens, you raise

your energy vibration, and

strengthen yourself and the

immediate energy field.

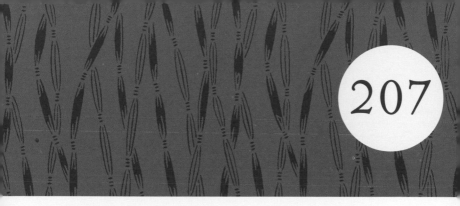

When you meet anyone, treat the event as a holy encounter. Nothing can be accomplished without relating positively to others.

e on the lookout for the

opportunity to say to yourself:

I feel good. I intend to attract more

of this good feeling, and I intend

to give it away to any and all

in need of it.

Your sense of awe with respect to all the miracles you perceive around you allows you to think, see, and live more of these miraculous occurrences. In contrast, a state of ingratitude stops this infinite flow.

If you're experiencing

scarcity, anguish, depression,

an absence of love—or any

inability to attract what you

desire—seriously look at how

you've been drawing these

circumstances into your life.

God is the mind through which you think and exist. It's always connected to you, even if you don't believe in it. Even an atheist doesn't have to believe in God to experience God.

212

When you're in a state

of joy and happiness, you've

returned to the pure, creative,

blissful, nonjudgmental joy

that intention truly is.

The universal mind was and is formless—it's the pure energy of love, beauty, kindness, and creativity, and it can't die—there's no form, no death, no boundaries, no deterioration, no flesh, and no possibility of it wasting away.

214

When you're inspired,
you activate dormant
forces, and the abundance
you seek in any form
comes streaming
into your life.

Universal Spirit is at work peacefully, and your attempts to rush it or tug new life into full creative flower will destroy the entire process. So trust in this wisdom to move at its own pace, and make no demands upon it.

Be aware that learning
to identify ways in which
you're creating your
own obstacles can
be tremendously
enlightening.

Involve yourself in high-energy levels of trust, optimism, appreciation, reverence, joy, and love when you engage in every activity in your life.

One of the most effective means for transcending *ordinary* and moving into the realm of *extraordinary* is saying *yes* more frequently and eliminating *no* almost completely. It's basically *saying yes to life.*

Think the best of everyone in your world. When you do so, you'll find that those positive thoughts come back to you in kind.

When you examine stress-producing incidents, you always have the choice to stay with thoughts that produce anxiety within you, or to activate thoughts that make it impossible.

*E*ven when nothing
seems to indicate that
you're accomplishing what
you desire in your life,
refuse to entertain doubt.

222

You must *be what it is* that you're seeking—that is, you always need to put forth what you want to attract.

When you feel good,

you're connected to

the power of intention,

regardless of what goes

on around you or what

others expect you to feel.

Picture the people in your
family with whom you're not
at peace, and feel the peace
you crave for them. Your inner
dialogue will change, and
you'll begin to experience
the relationships you desire.

Your purpose is between you and your Source, and the closer you get to what that field of intention looks and acts like, the more you'll know that you're being purposefully guided.

Act as if what you intend
to manifest in life is
already a reality.

*N*ight and day, dream of what you intend to do and what you intend to be, and those dreams will interpret your intentions. Let no doubt creep into your dreams and intentions.

The higher your energy field resonates, the more you're able to impact others with your own healing energy.

You won't recognize your genius aspect if you've been conditioned to believe that you should accept your lot in life, think small, and not aim too high in order to avoid disappointment.

*B*eing offended creates the same destructive energy that offended you in the first place— so transcend your ego and stay in peace.

Prayers, paintings, crystals, statues, spiritual passages in books, the colors on your walls, and even the arrangement of your furniture can all create energy that lifts you up rather than brings you down.

Find something to enjoy
in all fields of human and
creative endeavors, and
always work on expanding
your own horizons.

Engage in activities with high-energy fields, such as attending lectures on spirituality, taking yoga classes, giving or receiving massages, visiting monasteries or meditation centers, and volunteering or helping others in some way.

In every moment of your life, remember that every thought you have impacts you.

$\mathcal{E}$ach morning, affirm:

I attract only peace into my life.

When you do so, people will

respond to you with smiles,

acknowledgments, friendly

gestures, and kind greetings

all day long.

236

*C*hoose to see death
as simply removing a
garment or moving from
one room into another—
it's merely a transition.

Do not give mental energy to what others feel about how you should live your life. This can be a tough assignment at first, but you'll welcome the shift when it happens.

The qualities of creativity
and genius are within you,
awaiting your decision
to match up with the
power of intention.

If you really want approval, stop thinking about yourself, and focus on reaching out and helping others.

*T*ruly believe in the potential

for humans to live in peace and

be receptive to all, and you'll

be someone who's at peace and

receptive to life's possibilities.

You cannot remedy anything by condemning it. You only add to the destructive energy that's already permeating the atmosphere of your life.

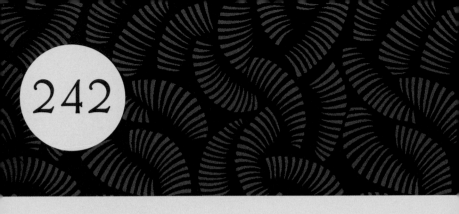

242

*R*emain confident that
through continued reliance
on your imagination,
your assumptions are
materializing into reality.

*W*ithin you is an infinite, passionate soul that wishes to express itself. It's the God within you, urging you to fulfill a deep sense of what you were meant to be.

244

Eternity is now! Right now, right here, you're an infinite being. Once you get past the fear of death as an end, you merge with the infinite and feel the comfort and relief that this realization brings.

Look upon every experience you've ever had, and everyone who has ever played any role in your life, as having been sent to you for your benefit.

You have the ability
to match up with the
power of intention and
attract ideal people and
divine relationships into
your life.

Look in the mirror at least once every day, and give thanks for the heart that continues to beat and the invisible force on which those heartbeats depend.

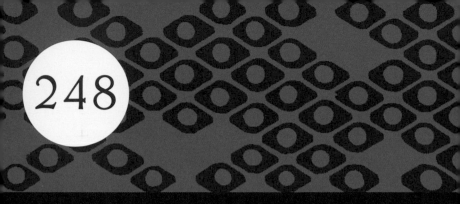

Being receptive means allowing your "Senior Partner" to handle your life for you.

*E*xtremely low-energy thoughts are evident if you use every conversation as an excuse to talk about yourself. Any behavior similar to this displays ego-dominated energy that impacts others unpleasantly.

By being big enough to make amends with your so-called enemies, you'll respect yourself much more than prior to your acts of forgiveness.

There are no losers in a world where we all share the same energy source. All you can say on a given day is that you performed at a certain level in comparison with the levels of others.

Feeling that you don't belong or that you're in the wrong place can be due to a lack of self-respect. Respect yourself and your divinity by knowing that everyone belongs. This should never come into question.

Remember that at every single moment of your life, you have the choice to either be a host to God or a hostage to your ego.

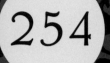

254

Start viewing the world by focusing on potentially optimistic viewpoints rather than on the negative prognostications of pessimists and "victims."

Be grateful for the abilities you've been given and the goods you've accumulated, but give all the credit to the power of intention, which brought you into existence and which you're a materialized part of.

Your feelings are clues about your destiny and potential, and they're seeking the full expression of life through you.

Your level of self-regard must come from knowing within yourself that you have a sacred connection. Let nothing shake that divine foundation.

Always be aware that you have the power to create the naturally stress-free and tranquil life you desire.

Be generous in all areas of your life. The more you give of yourself and all that flows to you, the more you'll see flowing back to you.

You don't need to work at *getting* healthy; health is something you already have if you don't disturb it.

By living in harmony
with Spirit, you need never
see yourself as separate. This
awareness is key to seeing
the power of intention
at work on a daily basis.

262

Don't make others' feelings about you more important than your opinion of yourself. If you've allowed any negative thoughts and opinions directed your way to become the basis of your self-portrait, you're asking the universal mind to do the same.

In any moment in which

you're experiencing thoughts

that make you feel sick or bad,

do your best to change them

to thoughts that support

the idea of feeling good.

When you eliminate the concept of separation from your thoughts, you begin to feel your connection to everything and everyone. You have a sense of belonging, which enables you to scoff at any thought of being separate.

Resist the inclination to assess others on the basis of their appearance, achievements, and possessions.

266

You live in a universe that

has limitless potential for joy

built into the creation process.

Your Source, the universal

mind of intention, adores

you beyond anything you

can possibly imagine.

Write down positive affirmations and read them on a regular basis. The act of writing will imprint these thoughts on your brain and have a long-lasting effect.

268

You get what you intend to create by being in harmony with the power of intention, which is responsible for all of creation.

Let go of the idea that you're a body that's destined to die, and instead seek an awareness of your immortal self.

*B*e proactive. Stay alert
for signs of synchronicity,
and never ignore them.

Your creative impulses are real, vital, worthy, and they crave expression. The fact that you can conceive of them is proof of this.

Affirm: *I am eternal, and that means that I showed up here from the infiniteness of spiritual intention to fulfill a destiny that I must act on.*

When you apply your unique individuality to tasks, you'll find that you can create anything you place your attention and imagination upon.

274

Know that everything
will happen at just the
right time, at just the
right place, with just
the right people.

Say "I want to feel good"
when you're tempted to
indulge in low-energy
thoughts.

View obstacles as opportunities to circulate the power of your unbending intent. This means being at peace, detaching yourself from the circumstances, and seeing yourself as the observer rather than the victim.

Leave your reputation for others to debate; it has nothing to do with you. Or as a book title says: *What You Think of Me Is None of My Business!*

Genuinely feeling successful is possible when you detach yourself from the things you desire and allow them to flow to you—and *through* you.

Harsh, pounding, musical vibrations with repetitive, loud sounds lower your energy level and weaken you and your ability to make conscious contact with intention.

Your idea that this is all temporary and that you aren't a piece of God's infinite perfection can lead you to self-doubt, anxiety, self-rejection, and depression. All it takes is a shift to infinite awareness to leave that misery behind.

Revenge, anger, and hatred are exceedingly low energies that keep you from matching up with the attributes of the universal force.

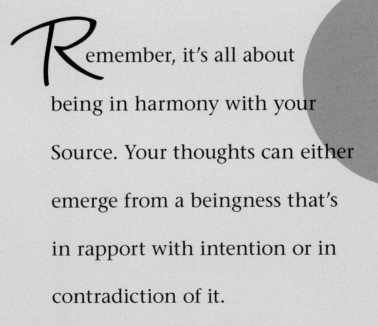

Remember, it's all about being in harmony with your Source. Your thoughts can either emerge from a beingness that's in rapport with intention or in contradiction of it.

Always find something to appreciate, whether it's the beauty of a starry night, a frog on a lily pad, a laughing child, or the natural radiance and splendor of the aged.

284

Since your Source is
always serving and giving
and you are your Source,
then you must always
be in a state of serving
and giving.

When you think, feel, and act kindly, you hasten your ability to connect to the power of intention.

When you're connected to the power of intention, you'll actually think and feel that any current disease pattern has never been present, and that you're already healed.

Make giving a way of
life. It is, after all, what
your Source and nature
do eternally.

e aware of your infinite

connection to your Source.

Know that you're more than

an encapsulated collection of

bones, blood, and organs in a

skin- and hair-covered body.

When you stop needing more of everything, more of what you desire seems to arrive in your life.

Self-important superiority

causes you to be constantly

offended in one way or another.

This misidentification is the

source of most of your problems,

as well as most of the

problems of humankind.

The effect of being in the

presence of people expressing

high frequencies is to feel

unified and connected to all of

nature and to all of humankind,

as well as the power of

intention.

Whatever attitude you have

about the world in general is

a good indicator of the respect

you have for your abilities

to intend into this world

what you desire.

You can't attract attractive-ness into your life by hating anything about what you've allowed yourself to become. Why? Because hatred creates a counterforce of hatred that disempowers your efforts.

294

*R*ealize how little you

need in order to be

satisfied and

at peace.

If you become what you think about, and you're thinking about what's wrong with the world and how angry, ashamed, and fearful you are, it stands to reason that you'll act on those thoughts and become what you're thinking about.

$\mathcal{E}$liminate thoughts of
conditions, limitations,

or the possibility

of something not

manifesting.

Simply trust your ability to cheerfully rely upon Spirit to express itself through and for you.

There's no actual stress
or anxiety in the world;
your thoughts create these
false beliefs.

Keep a solid picture of
the task you want to
accomplish in your mind,
and refuse to let that
intention disappear.

Stay in balanced harmony with the field of intention to help stabilize and harmonize the forces of the universe that can get out of balance when you live from a place of excessive ego.

Be unattached to all
who come into your life
by not demanding that
they stay, go, or appear
at your whim.

302

By making a conscious decision to distract yourself from worry, you've inaugurated the process of stress reduction, while simultaneously reconnecting to the field of all-creating intention.

Self-respect should be a natural state for you, just as it is for all of the animal kingdom. There's no raccoon out there that believes itself unworthy of what it intends to have!

Activating intention means rejoining your Source and becoming a modern-day sorcerer, which means attaining the level of awareness where previously inconceivable things are possible.

All stressful thoughts represent a form of resistance you wish to eradicate. Change those thoughts by monitoring your feelings and opting for joy rather than anxiety.

Know that the right people, things, jobs, books, pets—everything—will arrive to assist you in every aspect of your life.

People driven by the power

of intention have a strong

will that won't permit

anything to interfere

with achieving their

inner desire.

Know this: You can't expect to draw people into your life who are kind, confident, and generous if you're thinking and acting in cruel, weak, and selfish ways.

You aren't the elements that make up your body; you merely make use of the elements. You go beyond space and time and are merged with the infinite universal mind.

You don't need another diet, workout manual, or personal trainer. Go within, listen to your body, and treat it with all the dignity and love that your self-respect demands.

When the supremacy of ego is weakened in your life, you can then seek the power of intention and maximize your potential.

Look for something to appreciate in others, and be willing to communicate it to them and anyone else who's willing to listen.

Remind yourself every day of your infinite nature. Staying on the active side of infinity and being aware of it continually will put you in a position to manifest your desires.

314

The more you give of
yourself, the more you
open the door for life
to pour in.

View all your goals and activities as functions of your imagination working, guiding, encouraging, and even pushing you in the direction that intention had for you while you were still in an unmanifested state.

316

Spirit gives life, and everyone on this planet has Spirit within them as an all-powerful force for good.

If a friendship or partnership requires the violation of your self and your dignity, it's not really a friendship.

You and your power of intention are not separate, so when you form a thought that's aligned with Spirit, you create a spiritual prototype that sets into motion the manifestation of your desires.

The higher up the scale you move toward actually being the embodiment of enlightenment and God consciousness, the more you can counterbalance low energies.

When you're an open door that's never closed to possibilities, you'll be totally receptive to the abundance that's always ceaselessly flowing.

The more aware you become of your inner dialogue, the sooner you'll be able to shift from a thought of *I resent what's missing* to *I intend to attract what I want and stop thinking about what I dislike.*

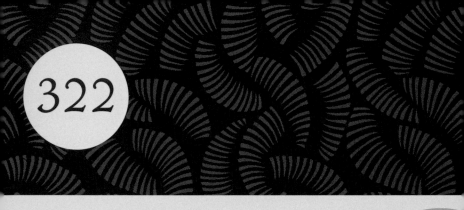

322

Everything and everyone in your personal history had to be there when they were. And what's the evidence for this? *They were there!* That's all you need to know.

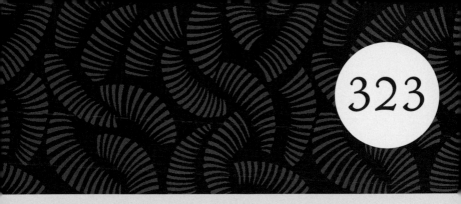

Be good to yourself.

You are God manifested,

and that's reason enough

to treat yourself kindly.

324

A simple thought of
forgiveness toward anyone
who might have angered you
in the past will raise you to the
level of Spirit and aid you in
your individual intentions.

Concerning abundance, one of the most effective ways to increase that pulling power from intention to you is to take the focus off dollars and place it on creating abundant friendship, security, happiness, health, and high energy.

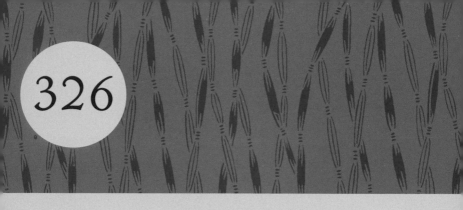

326

Your imagination is the concept of Spirit within you; it's the God within you. It's the invisible connecting link to manifesting your own destiny.

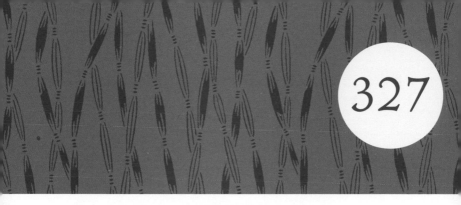

You have a one-of-a-kind
gift to offer this world,
and you are unique in the
entire history of creation.

llowing means that you

ignore efforts by others to

dissuade you. In an attitude of

allowing, all resistance in the

form of thoughts of negativity

or doubt is replaced with

simply knowing that you

and your Source are

one and the same.

Be thankful for the
wonderful gift of being
able to serve humanity,
your planet, and
your God.

330

You've been provided with a perfect body to house your inner invisible being. Regardless of its size, shape, color, or any imagined infirmities, it's a divine creation for the purpose that you were intended here for.

*U*nderstand your true essence, look death squarely in the face, and break the shackles of slavery to that fear. After all, *if you're not an infinite being, what would be the purpose of your life?*

Personal rewards multiply when you're focused on giving rather than receiving. Fall in love with what you're doing; and then "sell" that feeling of love, enthusiasm, and joy generated by your efforts.

Practice being in silence and meditation. Nothing relieves stress, depression, anxiety, and all forms of low energy more than that.

*E*go's idea of separation encourages you to base your worth on how frequently you emerge as a winner. As a hostage to your ego, self-respect is unavailable because you feel judged for your failures.

Make a decision to listen

carefully to your inner insights,

no matter how small or

insignificant you may have

previously judged them to be.

In a state of joy, you feel

fulfilled and inspired in all

facets of your life. In short,

gaining freedom from anxiety

and stress is a pathway to

rejoicing with the field

of intention.

It's impossible to ever

be disconnected from

the Source from which

you came.

Take no credit for your
talents, intellectual
abilities, aptitudes, or
proficiencies. Rather,
be in a state of awe
and gratitude.

You can feel purposeful every single day by taking a moment to cheer up a disgruntled employee, make a child laugh, or even pick up a piece of litter and place it in a trash can.

340

*R*efuse to talk about disease, and work to activate thoughts that predict recovery and overall well-being.

There's no such thing as luck

or accidents in this purposeful

universe. Not only is everything

connected to everything else,

but no one is excluded from

the universal Source

called intention.

342

Over and over, remind yourself: *I am not my body.*

I am not my accumulations.

I am not my achievements.

I am not my reputation.

I am whole and perfect as I was created!

Your call to purpose isn't necessarily about performing a specific task or being in a certain occupation. It's about sharing yourself in a creative, loving way using the skills and interests that are inherently part of you.

Release your need to feel superior by seeing the unfolding of Spirit in everyone.

The only thing that feeling bad accomplishes is to plummet you into anxiety, despair, depression, and stress. In such situations, ask yourself in that moment what thought you can have that will make you feel good.

Maintain a state of gratitude
and awe. Gratitude is the surest
way to stop the incessant inner
dialogue that leads you away
from the joy and perfection
of the Source.

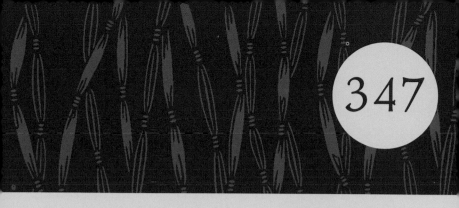

Make an internal

commitment to respect yourself

and to feel worthy of all that

the universe has to offer.

Disrespecting yourself is not

only disrespecting one of

God's greatest creations,

it's disrespecting God.

Move away from hoping, praying, and begging for the right people to show up in your life. Know that you have the power to attract them as long as you're able to shift from ego-driven energy to the all-providing Source of intention.

Listen carefully to your inner thoughts, no matter how small or insignificant you may judge them to be.

Inspiration comes from moving

back *in-Spirit* and connecting to

the power of intention. When

you feel inspired, what appeared

to be risky becomes a path you

feel compelled to follow.

Agitated thoughts that produce high blood pressure, a nervous stomach, persistent feelings of discomfort, an inability to sleep, and frequent displays of outrage are violating your natural state.

352

Meditation is a way to ensure that you stay in a state of self-respect. Regardless of all that goes on around you, when you enter into that sacred space of meditation, all doubts about your value as an esteemed creation dissolve.

Monitor your inner dialogue, and match your thoughts to what you want and what you intend to create.

354

Your imagination creates the inner picture that allows you to *participate* in the act of creation. It's the invisible connecting link to manifesting your own destiny.

*E*veryone is a child of God—everyone! Try to see this even in those who behave in what appears to be a godless fashion.

By giving authentic thanks for all the good you now have, as well as the challenges, you'll start the flow of *more* good into your life.

Simply by consuming low-energy substances, you'll find people with similar low energy showing up in your life. They'll want to buy those substances for you, party with you as you get high, and urge you to do it again after your body recovers.

*W*rite down the following affirmation, and repeat it over and over again to yourself: *I am the reflection of my Source, which is magnificent in all ways.*

Practice wanting for others what you want for yourself. In this way, everyone will benefit.

Sleep and dream of joy, and remember above all else: You feel good not because the world is right, but your world is right because you feel good.

Take constructive action
toward implementing
your inner intuitive
inclinations.

362

Choose to be in close proximity
to people who are empowering,
who appeal to your sense of
connection to intention, who
see the greatness in you, and
who feel connected to God.

Highly realized people learn to *think from the end*—that is, they experience what they wish to intend before it shows up in material form.

364

If life is infinite, then this is not life. Grasping this concept will connect you permanently to the infinite Source of Creation that *intends* everything.

*R*emember: *When you change the way you look at things, the things you look at change.* How you perceive the world is an extremely powerful tool that will allow you to fully bring the power of intention into your life.

Wayne W. Dyer, Ph.D., is an internationally renowned author and speaker in the field of self-development. He's the author of 30 books, has created many audio programs and videos, and has appeared on thousands of television and radio shows. His books *Manifest Your Destiny, Wisdom of the Ages, There Is a Spiritual Solution to Every Problem,* and *The New York Times* bestsellers *10 Secrets for Success and Inner Peace, The Power of Intention,* and *Inspiration* have all been featured as National Public Television specials.

Dyer holds a doctorate in educational counseling from Wayne State University and was an associate professor at St. John's University in New York.

Website: **www.DrWayneDyer.com**

○○○

NOTES

○○○

We hope you enjoyed this Hay House Lifestyles book.
If you'd like to receive a free catalog featuring additional
Hay House books and products, or if you'd like information
about the Hay Foundation, please contact:

Hay House, Inc.
P.O. Box 5100
Carlsbad, CA 92018-5100

(760) 431-7695 or **(800) 654-5126**
(760) 431-6948 (fax) or **(800) 650-5115 (fax)**
www.hayhouse.com® • **www.hayfoundation.org**

○○○

Published and distributed in Australia by: Hay House Australia Pty. Ltd.,
18/36 Ralph St., Alexandria NSW 2015 • *Phone:* 612-9669-4299
Fax: 612-9669-4144 • www.hayhouse.com.au

Published and distributed in the United Kingdom by: Hay House UK,
Ltd., 292B Kensal Rd., London W10 5BE • *Phone:* 44-20-8962-1230
Fax: 44-20-8962-1239 • www.hayhouse.co.uk

Published and distributed in the Republic of South Africa by:
Hay House SA (Pty), Ltd., P.O. Box 990, Witkoppen 2068
Phone/Fax: 27-11-706-6612 • orders@psdprom.co.za

Published in India by: Hay House Publishers India, Muskaan Complex,
Plot No. 3, B-2, Vasant Kunj, New Delhi 110 070 • *Phone:* 91-11-4176-1620
Fax: 91-11-4176-1630 • www.hayhouseindia.co.in

Distributed in Canada by: Raincoast, 9050 Shaughnessy St.,
Vancouver, B.C. V6P 6E5 • *Phone:* (604) 323-7100
Fax: (604) 323-2600 • www.raincoast.com

○○○

Tune in to **HayHouseRadio.com**® for the best in
inspirational talk radio featuring top Hay House authors!
And, sign up via the Hay House USA Website to receive the
Hay House online newsletter and stay informed about what's
going on with your favorite authors. You'll receive bimonthly
announcements about: Discounts and Offers, Special Events,
Product Highlights, Free Excerpts, Giveaways, and more!
www.hayhouse.com®